*I*t is the morning of your life

and all your dreams are just beginning.

Welcome to the world, dear little one.

This is the story of:

_____

Compiled with love by:

_____

Date:

_____

ISBN 0-7683-2048-8
Text by Flavia and Lisa Weedn
Illustrations by Flavia Weedn
© Weedn Family Trust
www.flavia.com

Published in 1998 by Cedco Publishing Company.
100 Pelican Way, San Rafael, California 94901
For a free catalog of other Cedco® products, please write
to the address above, or visit our website: www.cedco.com

Printed in Hong Kong

The artwork for each picture is digitally mastered using acrylic on canvas.

A MEMORY BOOK OF BABY'S FIRST YEAR

Dear Little One

Flavia and Lisa Weedn
Illustrated by Flavia Weedn

Cedco Publishing Company • San Rafael, California

*T*he privilege of PARENTING is by far

the most sacred of all blessings.

It is a time when we embark upon a

MUTUAL JOURNEY of self-discovery,

as we open our hearts and gaze into

the eyes of a precious new life to love.

The innocence and purity of a baby reminds us that

we are here for a PROFOUND PURPOSE.

We hold in our arms a tiny, precious soul and are granted the

most important role of all – to nurture,

protect and comfort, to turn fears into hopes and

tender cries into SMILES.

Our voice becomes a blanket of safety, our gentle embrace

reveals the promise of unconditional love.

How very blessed are we, for in the process we learn the

true meaning of life itself.

As we witness our child's first coos, first sighs,

first cries, we experience our instinctual heart reaching out,

only to find the glory of love reaching back for us.

There can be no finer gift, no greater miracle.

This journal is designed to become a

treasure-filled book, a legacy of love

to be passed from one GENERATION to the next.

When you finally close its pages, you'll hold in your hands

a golden thread of time . . .

the first chapter to the story of

your CHILD'S LIFE.

Flavia

Table of Contents

Our Family Tree

Sweet Beginnings

A Star Danced in Heaven

The Age of Innocence

My Firsts/My Discoveries

More Discoveries/More Firsts

My Favorite Things/My Favorite People

My Favorite Activities/Games and Stories

Special Family Times/Memories to Keep

So Big/My Growth Chart

Health Record/Staying Well

My Smile/Happy Times

A Time of Discovery

Discovering the World/Things that Excite Me

Finding Joy/Needing Comfort

Uniquely Me/Something to Say

Playmates/Caretakers

The Person I'm Becoming/My Personality

Standing Tall/My First Steps

My Hand Outline/My Foot Outline

An Artist's Touch/First Drawings

Anniversaries of the Heart

My First Holidays/Memorable Moments

My First Vacation/In Awe of the World

My First Birthday/Joy and Celebration

How Very Much I am Loved

Our Family Tree

Great Grandfather	Great Grandmother		Great Grandfather	Great Grandmother
Birthplace, Date	Birthplace, Date		Birthplace, Date	Birthplace, Date

Grandfather	Grandmother
Birthplace, Date	Birthplace, Date

Father

Birthplace, Date

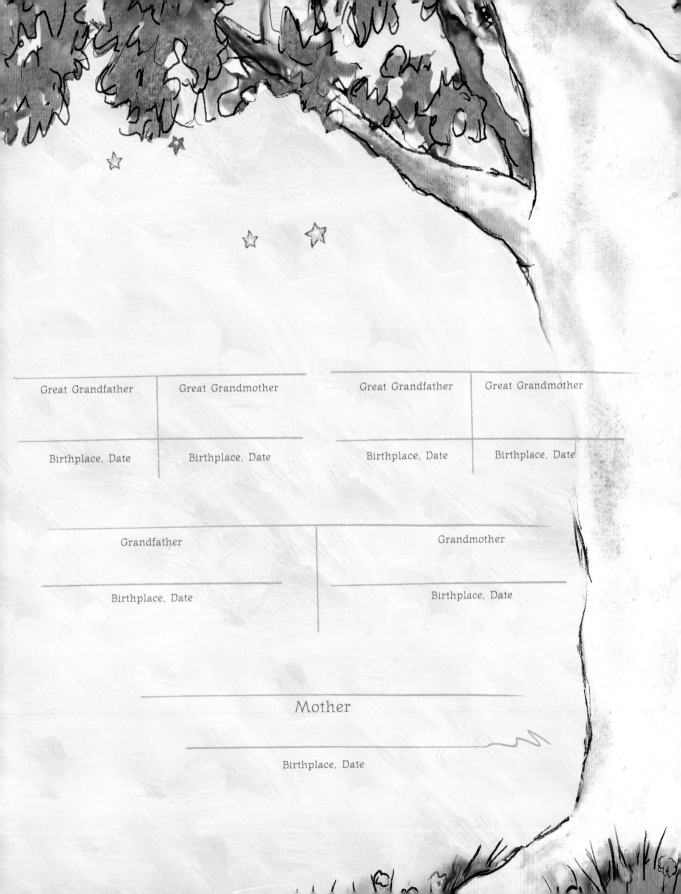

Great Grandfather	Great Grandmother	Great Grandfather	Great Grandmother
Birthplace, Date	Birthplace, Date	Birthplace, Date	Birthplace, Date

Grandfather	Grandmother
Birthplace, Date	Birthplace, Date

Mother

Birthplace, Date

Family History

Maternal Grandparents' story

Paternal Grandparents' story

Mama's Story

Love is the silver thread that connects the
dreams of our yesterday to the
miracles of our tomorrow.

Daddy's Story

Life

is a

series

of new

beginnings

and

wondrous

surprises.

Sweet Beginnings

he W I N D

offered *lullabies*

to the night sky,

while the **moon**

smiled *softly*

and waited

for a new baby

to arrive.

Hearing the News

A day to remember

Sharing the News

Loving reactions

Whispers of Love

Memories of pregnancy

_____

_____

_____

_____

_____

_____

_____

_____

Doctor visits, the ultrasound, exciting moments

_____

_____

_____

_____

_____

_____

_____

Before I was Born

Private conversations and music we listened to

_____

_____

_____

_____

_____

_____

Special times shared

_____

_____

_____

_____

_____

_____

_____

Celebrations

Baby shower(s)

Family and Friends

Dear friends and special gifts

Preparing the Nursery

My room awaits

Moments Before my Birth

What my parents were doing

$\mathcal{T}$he angels SANG

their praises and

a STAR DANCED

in heaven on the day

you were BORN.

The Day You Were Born

baby's full name

date   time

place

weight   length

Love at First Sight

_____

eye color   hair color

_____

who baby resembles

_____

who was there

_____

doctor/midwife   nurse

Precious One

tiny hands

date

little footprints

date

Keepsakes

hospital ID bracelet

birth announcement

First Moments

Memories of my birth

_____

_____

_____

_____

_____

_____

_____

_____

My parents' first words to me

_____

_____

_____

_____

_____

_____

_____

Tender Meanings

The meaning of my name

How my name was chosen

I Am Here

[paste birth certificate here]

First Images

[paste first photograph here]

Coming Home

Where we lived

_____

_____

_____

_____

_____

_____

Who was there to greet me

_____

_____

_____

_____

_____

_____

_____

Helping Hands

Visitors

_____

_____

_____

_____

_____

_____

_____

Caring hearts who helped

_____

_____

_____

_____

_____

_____

Joy and Elation

My first days

Trembling Hearts

My first nights

From the Heart

Gifts received

_____
_____
_____
_____
_____
_____
_____
_____
_____
_____
_____
_____
_____
_____
_____
_____

Welcoming Wishes

Cards and letters

Blessed Are We

Religious/spiritual ceremonies

When, where, and who was there

Gratitude and Praise

Prayers and blessings

My Godparents

Mama's Thoughts

Daddy's Thoughts

A child brings a special kind of love
into our hearts, and we are never, ever the same.

The Age of Innocence

$\mathcal{L}$OVE is a

guardian
angel

who is always nearby

protecting

and watching

over you.

My Firsts

Breast-feeding

First bath

First outing

Holding my head steady

Smiling and cooing

Laughing out loud

Rolling over

 Sitting up

My Discoveries

My favorite place to be

My favorite toy

Reaching for things

Reaching for Mama

Discovering my hands

Discovering feet and toes

Reaching for Daddy

Holding my bottle

More Discoveries

Where I like to sleep

My favorite lullaby

Sleeping through the night

What comforts me

Eating solid food

Playing peek-a-boo

Playing pat-a-cake

Holding cup and spoon

More Firsts

_____

First overnight journey

_____

First time without parents

_____

I can crawl

_____

First tooth

_____

First haircut

_____

First words

_____

First song

_____

First sentence

My Favorite Things

Objects of love and comfort

Toys, playthings and pets

My Favorite People

Who they are

What we do together

My Favorite Activities

Games and Stories

And

high

overhead

there are

millions

of stars

smiling,

looking

down, and

blessing

you.

Special Family Times

If we could sit across the porch from God,
we'd thank Him for lending us you.

Memories to Keep

So Big

My Weight at Birth

_____

	lbs	ounces			lbs	ounces
One Month				Seven Months		
Two Months				Eight Months		
Three Months				Nine Months		
Four Months				Ten Months		
Five Months				Eleven Months		
Six Months				Twelve Months		

Special Notes

_____

_____

_____

_____

_____

My Growth Chart

My Height at Birth

inches   inches

One Month _____   Seven Months _____

Two Months _____   Eight Months _____

Three Months _____   Nine Months _____

Four Months _____   Ten Months _____

Five Months _____   Eleven Months _____

Six Months _____   Twelve Months _____

Special Notes

_____

_____

_____

_____

_____

_____

_____

Health Record

Date	Doctor	Reason for Visit	Comments

Special Notes

Staying Well

Date	Immunization	Reaction

Special Notes

My Smile

From gummy smiles
to my first teeth...

Date   Age   Which Tooth

Trips to the Dentist

Happy Times

Childhood

is an

enchanted

place

in the

heart.

 child

fills a **sacred** place

INSIDE our *hearts*,

a place

we never knew

was empty.

A Time of Discovery

Discovering the World

A child lives in the land of discovery,

and dances in the land of make-believe.

Things that Excite Me

Finding Joy

What makes me laugh

Needing Comfort

What makes me cry and how I'm soothed

Uniquely Me

My mannerisms and
how I earned my nicknames

Something to Say

Caretakers

If while you are a child
just one someone loves you uncritically,
then you will have love to give
for the rest of your life.

The Person I'm Becoming

My Personality

To
be
a child
is to believe
in wonder,
to believe
in angels
and fairies
and the
man in
the moon.

Standing Tall

Standing up

My First Steps

Walking on my own

My Hand Outline

My Foot Outline

_____ Date

An Artist's Touch

Date

First Drawings

Date

Anniversaries

of the

Heart

These are the days

to REMEMBER,

to cherish

and hold forever

DEEP within

the heart.

My First Holidays

Memorable Moments

Into some hearts love brings a little heaven.

My First Vacation

Sweet

baby...

our life.

our love.

our joy.

In Awe of the World

My First Birthday

Joy and Celebration

When we think of all the things that
would have never been, if *you* had never been,
we celebrate the day you were born.

How Very Much

A letter from Mama

I am Loved

A letter from Daddy

Photo by Claudia Kunin

Flavia Weedn is one of America's leading contemporary inspirational writers and illustrators. Her work has touched the lives of millions for over three decades. Offering a kind of hope for the human spirit, Flavia portrays the basic excitement, simplicity and beauty she sees in the ordinary things of life. Lisa Weedn, Flavia's daughter and co-author, shares her mother's philosophy and passion. Their collaborative writings celebrate life and embrace meaningful core values. It is their wish to shine a beacon of hope into the lives of others by encouraging the belief that we all have a significant contribution to make in this lifetime and every dream can be realized. Their work includes numerous books, collections of fine stationery goods, giftware, and lifestyle products distributed worldwide. Flavia and Lisa live in Santa Barbara, California.